Honouring

Our

Veterans

2013

Copyright © 2013

This book was completed with the volunteer efforts of Joe Robinsmith, whose poetry book *"Heartsongs from a Cowboy's Soul"* was published in April 2011.

Maple Ridge
Christian School
12140 - 203 Street
Maple Ridge BC V2X 2Z5

Dedication

This book of poetry is a collection of the poems submitted during the 3rd Annual Honouring Our Veterans Poetry contest. This contest was organized by Joe Robinsmith in Maple Ridge, BC with the support and sponsorship of The Maple Ridge-Pitt Meadows Times Newspaper.

Major sponsors of this event without whom the contest would not have succeeded are:

Maple Ridge Pitt Meadows Times
Maple Ridge Mayor Ernie Daykin
Black Bond Books
MP Randy Kamp

I would especially like to thank the following people:

Roxanne Hooper - MRPM Times Newspaper
Shari Craig – Black Bond Books
Rhonda Vance – Blossmmms Specialty Cupcakes

Sincerely,

Joe Robinsmith

Will There Ever Be Peace? © Mary Tanco

Will there ever be peace has been asked many times before
Till threats of conflicts cease forever more
It is with heartbreaks that countries can not get along
It would be just as easy to try to belong

Greed and religion may be the cause of strife and sorrow
Because most want to spend and borrow
Once money runs out countries demand more
To pay it back takes many a score

Waiting for payment countries become restless ready for a
fight
While young recruits hold fort with all their might
Weapons of mass destruction can be used secretly hidden
If found they quickly become forbidden

Land mines are another hazard of war being used to even
an unpaid score
To protect the country many lives are lost
In the name of security and human cost
God's will was peace on earth goodwill to men

If we follow that advice we'll have peace only then
November 11th is the day to remember
Those who sacrificed their life for our freedom
So we can participate in memory of our loved ones
heavenly home.

Webster's Corner Elementary Poetry

Veterans Poem - Harmony Kline

Many soldiers fought to keep us safe
they risked there lives for us
they tried their hardest
they were feeling sad trying to save our country
everything they had has been destroyed houses, buildings, places
being bombed even some of the families were bombed.
Soldiers being shot and adults and kids leaving to go somewhere
safe.

Veterans Poem - Courtney Holm

It happens everywhere, every day, every month, every year.
In many different places Germany, France, Greece, Sweden, so
many different places think of all how die, the pain, the anger
that you have been shot and then yell (man down) and you look
over and you see your friends are running to your aid,
the feeling that you are going to be saved it is the best that soon
you will be home with your family,
you are fighting for you country
you are making a differences
You are a hero.

Veterans Poem - Blake Klassen

Marching to fight the enemy
Rattling of chains on the ground
The smell of burning ash
My heart pumping from adrenaline
They are listing to there leader
Marching home to go see are families

Veterans Poem - Lochlinn Ireland

The violence of world war 2
The frightening look of terror
Hear the people screaming and feeling their pain
I can see their pain
I can smell blood and gun powder and rotting flesh
I see flies all over the bodies

Veterans Poem - Cache Talson-Urquhart

In the battlefield I hear gunshots and bombs going off,
I see bodies everywhere,
I smell death all around me.
I feel scared, the cold gun under my chin.
The taste of dust in my mouth.
I wish I were home.

Veterans Poem - Colby Soolsma

The USS Missouri ready for war.
I see the aftermath of a bombing.
There is smoke everywhere.
I see fear every direction I look.
Here comes Hitler's army.
I see a lot of men behind him.
I smell and see ash everywhere.
I look up and see a bomb coming right at me.

War – Zoe Olson

Imagine this picture:
you see man holding his child
Maybe he hasn't seen that child in months
he has sacrificed spending time with his child
instead he has been fighting for the child's freedom and for
a good life
he knows that if he wins this his child will have a good life
and his son or daughter's children will have good life
and everyone after.
This man is willing to give his life for everyone.
That is what the war can make you do.

Veterans Poem – Houston Horton-Griffis

I see tanks and hear the footsteps of the enemy convoy.
I taste dirt and smell death all around me.
I feel scared.
I hear the screams of people all around.
I hear the roar of planes in the distance.
I feel the cold metal of my gun.
I am scared, so I camp.

War - Danny Thai

War
Heavy hearted family's
Soldiers in fear
Women and children evacuated,
all in tears
Warriors in battle
Families broken
All for us
Thank you

Veterans Poem – Samantha Barnier

If I was in a war, I would be totally scared.
Maybe it's a bad guy or maybe it's a good guy.
I would hear bombs dropping and screaming probably.
Maybe there is a happy moment because it looks like they just
won land.
It is windy and crowded.
Maybe people were even getting thrown off the boat.
 a lot of bombs dropping and people dying,
and people screaming for their lives.
You can explain it by being scary, loud, sad.
People would definitely be crying, they would definitely be
scared.
If I were there, I would never want to leave my parents.

Those Soldiers – Kiarah Smith

The world war was very sad.
Many died each day maybe even more than once a day.
Kids got sent away to be safe.
Bombing happened all the day everyday.
People never got to see their families again.
Most didn't make it but all fought for our country and our rights.
Remember those solders who fought for us and our freedom
today.

War – Sarah Weber
(3rd Place Elementary Category)

We Wear A Poppy On Our Chests
To Represent The Soldiers That Were Put To Rest.
They Were Strong And Must Have Had Big Hearts
Because They Risked Their Lives To Help Their Country Stay
Alive.
When It Comes to The Time For Them To Leave
We Will Remember Them and Hope They Rest. In. Peace

The Man In The Tank – Conrad Brierley

Every thing is falling apart
I Hear gunshots but mostly silent
It smells like dust and fumes
Tastes like grit and a metal
It feels safe that I am in a tank and happy I am not dead

WWII Poem – Jaidon Scott

Old, dirty, a different time.
Old, frail, small, tube like.
Men fly to their death perhaps.
Not the smartest.
A shotgun against a tank?
War is crazy!
A nice turret, littered with casings.
Who's on the other side?

World War 2 – Corbin Ray

Charging into battle
Take the tank to the fight
Raise the flag to honor the country
Stop the enemy no matter what
The warriors of freedom have landed

War – Lexi Askew
(3rd Place Elementary Category)

War Isn't just fighting
War Isn't just kill before you get killed
War Is fighting for something you believe in
War Is losing someone you love
The soldiers that go to war don't go just to kill
They don't go just because they have to
They go, because once their in there's no going back
And they fight for something they all believe in
They fight to protect their loved ones
They never give up No matter how much it may hurt
They will never leave a man behind
War Is something we should avoid
War Is something that can kill us all
It tears our world apart It makes countries turn on one another
War Is full of hatred and want
There should be no more war
Will be the end of humanity and civilization
I want one thing
And one thing only
And that is.......
To say goodbye to war forever

World War 2 Poem – Isaac Harris

I hear the gun blasting
running into war
Commanding all the solders
Tired but trying my best not to give up
Marching through the mud
The smell of smoke
The U.S won the war

Veterans Poem – Maggie Tomlinson

Think about Those soldiers who fought for you
they risk their lives for yours.
Some of them died and never saw their family again.
They lived for the rest of their lives with no mom or dad.
Their houses got bombed and they were homeless
started to not have enough food to feed their family.
Many soldiers fought to keep us safe.

WWII – Paige Beadell

War is Cold
War is bare
when it is over no one is there the British are gone
the Spanish Have fallen
the wrong thing is when the go
when they go the world is sad
those family's are sad because their loved ones wer killed
the German got though and shout the people
and tanks came and boomed the people's houses
and kill many people who lived where slaves
even kids, even the sick, the wounded people and no mans land
though that they had gave up
but then they looked up and no one was there
they saw tracks and guns all over the place
War is bad no more war

World War 2 Poem – Isaac Harris
I hear the gun blasting
running into war
Commanding all the solders
Tired but trying my best not to give up
Marching through the mud
The smell of smoke
The U.S won the war

World War 2 Poem – Hudson Costa

World War 2 was a sad time for others.
For brothers and sisters and fathers and mothers.
From 1939 to 1945, many soldiers died,
only some left alive.
Germany attacked Poland, to start off the war.
Many annihilated, both rich and poor.
Then Germany surrender to end the big fight.
To the Soviet Union, now everyone's all right.
Families were lost. Soldiers were too.

WW2 poem. – Hudson Carruthers

WWII was probably the saddest time for people all around
the world. Soldiers fought hard and they didn't stop,
they didn't give up, they kept fighting for their country.
These were years of fighting in freezing cold conditions
where their fingers were falling off from frostbite
and then being told to go out and fight in snow up to their
waist. Sometimes sleeping in muddy trenches with no
blankets or pillows. They also fought in the boiling hot
dessert
or marching in the jungle at night
knowing that at any second Japanese troops could jump out
of the bush and kill you without any one seeing.
Constantly bullets wising by your head,
and bombs falling everywhere!
I don't know many people brave enough to do all that.

War is No Place for Anyone – Rebecca Franklyn
(2nd Place Adult Category)

When the guns salute,
and the airplanes roar,
and the bagpipes play,
and the children sing,

Memories hidden deep,
surge forth,
again.

Wounds that once were torn,
reopen,
bleed,
and re-scar the earth.

The dead soldiers whisper,
remember what war was like,
and how it hasn't changed?

So then…

Why do we still hate?
Why do we still fight?
Why do we still kill?

Should we not,

Stand strong against war,
be the change,
be the peace,
and Remember.

What are we still fighting for?

How many lives has it wrecked?
Torn apart,
Destroyed.

Stand strong against war,
be the change,
bring peace,
and Remember.

Our soldiers died for peace.
Should we not honour them?
Should we not *honour* them?
And end our wars.

Let their memories be *remembered*.
Let them be the *heroes* they were.
Let their sacrifices *mean* something.

Because those who died fighting,
want to have died for a cause,

Stand strong against war,
be the change,
bring peace,
and Remember.

Do not forget them,
or what they gave our country.

Let us remember them on Remembrance Day.
Let us be their freedom.
Let us be their peace.

War is no place for anyone.

The Soldier Who Came Home – Marlowe Evans
(1ˢᵗ Place Secondary Category)
A soldier sat waiting.
The enemy came- a shot pierced the darkness.
The bullet hit true,
and the soldier fell to his knees:
overcome by the realization
of what he had done:
he had taken a life-
the first of many.

The pattern continued…
a pattern of darkness and bloodshed,
until finally the fight was over;
it was time to go home.

When the soldier returned,
his children had grown,
his brother had died.
The world had changed without him.
The thing he needed most: to talk,
to have someone understand the lives he'd taken.
But no one would listen to his nightmares or his sadness,
so they stayed heavy in his heart.

We remember those who died,
with poppies on our hearts,
but we forget the living.
The soldiers who survived war,
they remember death
more intensely than anyone could know.
The next time we think of Flanders Fields:
remember not only those
who rest below the swaying poppies-
but remember who fought,
and lived-
The soldier who came home.

Simple Words Honouring our Veterans
© Hélène Levasseur

Tis' with awe and glory that we salute you lovingly
Wearing the Flanders' Poppy with respect and dignity
Because of our veterans we live in a protected country
And pray for peace on earth and goodwill to all man.

Your flamboyant style and distinguished eloquence
Makes us realize that you have given your life purpose
To ascertain the preservation of ours forever and ever
Our veterans dead or alive pray and work for us incessantly

November the 11th is the Parade and is full of celebrations
Where we collectively assemble all Canadians thanking
Our admirable veterans for their skills and dedication
Diligently shared overcoming any fears or tribulations.

Many thanks to all veterans past, present and future
Wear your beret with effervescent glory and harmony
In your presence we feel safe, secure and gratified
Because of you we live with a hopeful mentality.

Song Dedication

I wrote this song as a dedication to my Great Grandfather
Roy Munro and his brothers who fought in WW I.
According to my Grandmother, my Great Grandfather Roy
Munro and his brothers all lived in the Popkum-Rosedale
area of B.C. and fought in WW I. The War had devastating
effects on them all. Roy Munro fought in the battle of
Vimy Ridge and was injured, his brother Stan Munro had
his left arm blown off and suffered the rest of his life from
shell shock. Roy's brother Frank was killed in the War and
Roy's other brother Zeph was too young to enlist so he
travelled to England to aid the war effort from there. I have
often wondered what it would have been like for my
grandfather and his brothers and their parents to go through
such a horrific experience as a world war and the horrors of
trench life and trench warfare. I can only imagine the
importance of letters between soldiers and their families. It
is with the deepest respect I dedicate this song to them.
Sincerely, Darren Morrey

Trees To Trenches – Darren Morrey
(1ˢᵗ Place Adult Category)
Mom and Dad, did you know? Did you know?
From climbing trees to a trench I'd go,
Wet behind the ears no more, no more.
I've seen it all, I have seen war,
And my heart it longs for home,
Passchendaele has stolen my soul.

And here I stand in no man's land,
With mud and blood on every man.
So I seal it in this letter I send.
Remember me, and this Great War

To end all wars so they say.
Will they remember me and the price I pay?
Mom and Dad, did you know? Did you know?
From climbing trees to a trench I'd go,
Wet behind the ears no more, no more.
I've seen it all, I have seen war,
And my innocence is gone,
Lost at Vimy and the Somme.

But here I am with gun in hand,
Over the top I march again.
The fog of Ypres burns like sand.
Remember me and this Great War
To end all wars so they say.
Will they remember me and the price I pay?

Mom and Dad, did you know? Did you know?
From climbing trees to a trench I'd go,
Wet behind the ears no more, no more.
I've seen it all, I have seen war.

Remember – Sherine Stanyer

Sixty eight years have past, since our brave Veterans risked their lives for
our freedom.
And the horrific memories of suffering and losses still last.
Where many crosses mark the graves of brave men.
The Mothers, Children, and Wives who had to carry on,
despite their losses.
The work keeps running through my head,
"Why, Why, Why did they have to die?"
And I remember, it was written, man will destroy himself
by his own hand.
Greed, Control, and Power is what it was all about.
On November 11th we will have a moment of silence, to remember years of
suffering and losses.
So buy those poppies, and wear them proud.
By now we have lost many of our surviving Veterans.
I am proud to be Canadian, and I hope Canada will always be a peace keeping
country.

Not My Baby – Erin Kieneker

The call rings out,
The people rush forth,
So eager to enlist,
From factories,
To far off places,
But I just clench my fists.

Not my baby.

I am not afraid,
I want to help,
I can't let evil win,
But I cannot let go,
I can barely move,
Let go of my baby, where to begin?

A strong and handsome man is he,
So brave to volunteer,
He looks so ready, so sure,
So unaware,
The tears I hold back,
Where is the baby that I held dear?

Not my baby.

I watch him go,
The hardest part,
When will I see him again?
At Christmas next?
Or heaven's gate?
How can my heart explain?

I keep my hands busy,

I do what I must,
Building and working all day,
But my minds never far,
From all I might loose,
The world does feel very grey.

Not my baby.

Distant memories of a little soft head,
Curled contentedly on my lap,
Sweet little laughter,
A heart full of joy,
My beautiful boy,
A delight to look after.

A knock at my door,
The fear in my chest,
An ugly beast
Who rips and who tears
A telegram, a flag, I fall to my knees
In a moment my heartbeat has ceased.

Not my boy.

So brave and so strong,
They say he died a hero.

Not my boy.

He was fighting for his country,
For you and for me.
His last breath, his last action,
Given to a greater cause.
Although I am proud,
I have little satisfaction.

Not my boy.

I will never see his big blue eyes again,
Or hold him in my arms,
But I remember.
And each and every man and women
who gave part of themselves
I remember.

I will never forget.
Not my boy.

No Glory in War – Jade Soon

His heart began to race and he could hear every accentuated
thump.
And the cold, the bone-chilling cold numbing his legs and
arms.
Every second felt like hours stretching well into the night.
On sentry duty, he watched intensely.. peering into the
night watching for any odd movement
Listening to any strange sound. Was the enemy as scared as
he was?
Out in the freshly dug trenches he began to reminisce about
the life he left in Canada.
Was it only weeks before that he was embraced by the love
of his family?
And now he huddled, shivering sharing the damp and
musty earth with huge nightcrawlers.
Inadequately clothed, he yearned for the comforts of a
home cooked meal and the security of family and friends.
Distraught he began to weep.
He was trying to be strong, he was trying to be brave
But no one could tell him how war really was.
No one told him about the cold damp nights, the loneliness
and the fear of the unknown.
War was not glorious, war was a living nightmare.

Deep down in the depths of his soul he wanted to run and never return.

What did his future hold? Would he make it home alive and if he did, would he ever be the same?

Yesterday's battle was horrific, men scattering as they shot at the enemy.

His comrades lay injured and amid the screams of pain and agony, he tried desperately to help.

This was not a time to be squeamish. He pressed hard on the broken, bloody arteries of his fellow wounded.

He cried out words of encouragement that everything would be alright.

Who could really understand the horrors of war?
Who could return to a peaceful life at home and erase the visons of mutilated bodies that lay on the battlefields?

Would Canadians really understand the sacrifice that these brave men and women faced in war?

There is no glory in war!

Maple Ridge Christian School Poetry

Thank You – Ciarra Van Dop

Thank you Veterans, for all your hard work
Thank you for fighting through mud and dirt
Thank you for being so brave
Thank you to the ones in the grave
It got colder - - - you got bolder
Thank you for making our country free
Thank you Veterans for everything you've done for me
This poem is hard to write, because it makes me think of
the terribly hard fight!
Thank you, so very much Veterans.

Time to Join – Dawson Ignatieff

Smoke filled the air as I stood there petrified
Though I never fired a gun, today it must be done
I couldn't join the war on out there
For I was much too scared.
The sound pierced my ears,
There was still pride in me
Which shall ride with me through this time.
It was time for me to join the war.
As I stepped on the field
My body was my only shield.
I don't want to be shot
But the war must be fought
'till this day soldiers like me
Are standing alive and free.
Wearing poppies over our heart
We have done our part

Freedom Is Never Free – Kendra Marginean

I hear the rifle's crack
Of the enemies attack

I walk the edge of the shore
And witness the bloody gore

This sea of red
Of soldiers now dead

They paid the greatest cost
With their lives --- now lost

I take careful aim with my scope
And see a new life filled with hope

I pray for peace
On my life's new lease

Our debts have been paid
By sacrifices that were made

Freedom is never free
We have a choice to be ---
What we can be ---

A Canadian Soldier – Elke Sorensen

A Canadian soldier risked his life
Leaving his family full of strife
The mother, the daughter, the newborn son
Waiting and praying for the war to be done.

A Canadian Soldier went off to war
Leaving his family fatherless and poor
Not enough money, just hunger and sadness
Because a war's full of worry, anger and madness.

A Canadian soldier came back full of life
Hugging and kissing, embracing his wife
No more hate and aggression, just peace
And a prayer that the armistice will never cease.

Freedom Is Not Free – Kaitlyn Lozinski

Freedom is not free
Remember veterans who died for freedom
Every soldier was willing --- to fight for freedom.
Eternal love for all who died.
Do you have griefs that we do not know of?
Oh Canada, we are a peace keeping country.
May the poppies remind us of every life.

I may never experience war because ---
Soldiers fought for us.

Let the poppies grow.
I thank you veterans
For all you have done.
Every veteran's soul in heaven rejoice.

Thank You – Caitlin Tolson

Thank you veterans for freeing us from war
Thank you God for making heaven
So all the soldiers who fought for us to be free
Could go to heaven and feel safe
No blood, no fear, no war
So they don't have to suffer any longer
Or feel any more pain.

Thank you Lord for healing the wounds
Of soldiers that weren't killed
And had to see terrible things
Even though they will never forget the things they have
seen

Thank you Lord for sending angels
To be there with all the soldiers
And people who had loved ones
That died to save us in battle.

On this Remembrance Day
Be thankful for everything that you have
Be thankful that Canada doesn't have war
We always have to be thankful
But we also have to pray for the veterans.

So remember that not all the world is free
Remember the poppies and be thankful
To all the veterans then and now for freeing us from war.

Remembrance Day Poem – Isaac Mrowka

The poppy is a good symbol of what you've done,
For when I'm older I can show my son
Even if you're in your grave,
There is memory of you in which we save,
But even if it fades away
The pride will forever stay.

Red and White – Keegan Prophet

Red and white
We shine bright
We strive for peace
Because we are free
The maple leave that stands on our flag
Shows a symbol of freedom to those that lag
We love those who fought for freedom
Anyone else to do the job, is just not right.
Those who were chosen had to die
To save all of our lives.
The poppies that we wear
Show that we care
We remember them with a minute of silence,
Gratitude, respect and thanks to the brave
The ghosts of the past
Show us we will last.
Red and white
We shine bright.

Remember Me – Shibayama Tsuchiya

I'm in a row with a thousand more
All standing straight, proud and tall
None ready for the terror of war
So let's hope its mild
Be with me.

I'm in the truck so cold and scared
With others around me
With fear in their eyes
All have guns at their sides and grenades
At their other
Protect Me

In the battlefield with others more
All ready to give up their lives
As the war began we all ran with
Flying hopes of winning
But suddenly in the chest I felt
The cold, metal bullet
As the world around me
Started turning white
I prayed a silent prayer that God would protect
The innocent and non-innocent lives of the fallen
Remember Me

Sacrifice – Emma Pollard

Soldiers brave and strong
Away from home
Cold and wet
Rode in tanks
Isolated and lonely
Fought for freedom
Independence and equality
Canada's best
Everyone remember their sacrifice

Words – Annika Meekel

Fight, kill destroy, attack shoot, battle
Military, struggle, combat, assault, hate.

- War

Friendship, truce, order, unity, serenity,
Calm, love.

- Peace

Freewill, independence, opportunity,
Liberty, rights, power, choices, Canada.

- Freedom
Thank you Veterans

Red and Black – Ethan May

Red is the color of the blood that the Veteran's gave
That now is trampled beneath their graves.
Blue is the colour of the water they drank
Although refreshed their hearts still sank
Pink is the colour of the morning sun,
That called them to rise for everyone
Black is the colour of the dark gloomy sky
That crushed the soldier's dream to fly.
White is the colour of the glistening snow,
That stopped the soldiers when they heard a blow
Yellow is the colour of the bright shining gold
That filled up their hearts, ever so bold.
Now red and black are the colours of the poppies worn today,
It shows the heroic deeds and the narrow getaways.

A Moment of Silence – Ehi Obetoh

A moment of silence is a time use to remember those who fought in the different wars to give us freedom to move around freely.

This should be used for something to honour those who fought in the wars.

BOOM ! CRASH ! SLAM ! These sounds can remind veterans of the gruesome and horrific sights that they saw. Different people have never seen peace, but we have never seen war.

We should respect those who went to war and fought for our freedom. Those who died and those who lived they all have a huge impact on our lives today.

PING ! BANG ! TRA-TAT-TAT ! These have different effects on everybody's life. Most bring back the bad things that happened in war.

In the trenches that they stayed were not the best places to live but they served their purpose and did their job. There were diseases that were passed around in there.

When a moment of silence is declared we shouldn't take it lightly. It is a time to remember those who sacrificed their lives for our freedom.

It's Time to Remember – Annika Piir
(2nd Place Elementary Category)

It's time to remember our brave soldier friends
For may, their lives would come to an end.

It's time to remember the sacrifice made
The memories of families and friends never fade.

It's time to remember the innocent ones,
Who died in the war without bearing guns,

It's time to remember those in their graves
Who fought for their country so bold and so brave

It's time to remember the poppies we wear
A visible sign we remember and care.

Veterans – Elliot Banbury

Valiant heroes chose to fight the
Endless war day and night
True heroes they were and are
Everywhere – they are not far
Remembering what they did for us
And knowing they're the ones we trust
Now where most are
Sleeping in the poppy field graveyard.

I Remember – Peter Madari

As I'm running from the guns that flash
I think back to the horrific past
The war was far from fun
I was terrified to shoot the gun
I remember the missiles crashing down beside me
I think back to when one struck my friend Darren McGee
These days I can't even keep a steady hand because I'm
nervous
And every Sunday morning I'm in service
I think back to that one day when we won
There we laid together as one.

I laid there till I saw the moon
Heading back home I though it was noon
Hopping in the place I heard someone call my name
I stood there in awe because it was the one and only God
He told me to not be afraid because tomorrow will be
another day
That was when I knew I would never forget that day
Even right now while I'm staring at the grave.

Veteran – Jacob Peterson

V ery brave and strong, each one
E ver serving our country with loyalty
T rying to forget the pain of war
E njoy our freedom today because of them
R emembering the past is important for us
A lways helps us and we benefit from vets
N ever is disloyal, so nor should we!

Remembrance Day – Callum Baaker

Crawling through the trenches alone
Scared and chilled to the bone
With home so many miles away
Our brave soldiers keep the enemies at bay
Each year we give thanks and honour
Displayed on our collar
The red poppy of courage we may
Proudly wear on Remembrance Day.

In Remembrance of Them – Kayleb Hough

No greater love for them to give
They fought for our freedom, so we could live.
The good book says this is the best
To lay one's life down for the rest.
Their commitment in life is ours to follow
To live a life of love, not hollow.
In remembrance of them.
We must do good to others,
For in this small world we're simply all brothers.

Day to Remember – Bonnie Roda
(3rd Place Adult Category)

D evastation, death, despair
A s justice promoters, we are humbled by the selfless
efforts of others on our behalf
Y et we gain only through the courageous ones who have
gone before us.

To gether we pray for God's mercy and wisdom

R ed , the colour of our poppies, like drops and splashes of
blood
E very soldier determined to be brave and strong
M other's hearts at home pounding with worry, hope and
persistent prayers.
E cclesastes 3:8 "There is a time to wee and a time to
laugh, a time to mourn and a time
    to dance, a time for war and a time for peace."
M arching, mourning, marching, mourning.
B rothers and sisters, sons and daughters, mothers and
fathers
E ver striving to give the gift of peace and a cold cup of
water
R est in the knowledge that your honourable sacrifice is
sincerely appreciated.

Left Behind – Wilhelmina Martin

Here I am for eternity. My essence left behind, seeped into the earth, my last breath on the wind.

I am a ghost of history. Left behind by failing memories of comrades, now aged and infirm.

Left behind by young, invincible generations obsessed with money, power,

Unable to look backward, for a glimpse of the price I paid for the course laid before me.

Left behind, I am a casualty of conflicts, old and new, the many and the few.

Left behind by families who mourned and then moved on. Replaced as father, brother, son by those who stayed, or who returned, some whole, many broken, with hollow eyes of horrors witnessed and grace withheld amid the pleadings, amid the dying moans of boys and men, calling for God, for mother and for salvation. And then, silence.

Yet I remain here to remind you, with a whisper, that tingling sensation as you rush by in this stairwell that someone, something, relevant, if only for a fraction of a millennial second, took place here in history. The hunter, the gladiator, the crusader, the warrior, we touch hands across the chasm of time: those who fight and are left behind.

This was inspired by the photograph by Jo Hedwig Teeuwise in Ghosts of History.

Ghosts of Remembrance © Janet Kvammen

Haunting memories
held tight in November's grasp
air gone chill
The autumn mourn
whispers her secrets
to a somber crowd

Spectral shadows
rise above stooped shoulders
A cloudy past clear as yesterday
The old vet's head held high
Medals weigh heavy on his heart

Poppies, ever red
float on sea of grey
Within each petal written
      a sacred elegy of respect
      a blessing of hope
      a prayer for peace

The only sound is silence
as a young girl
takes the hand of her grandfather
She smiles up at him
while he wipes a tear from his eye
Softy she says "Look, Grandpa, look,
the poppy I wear is for you!"

The November rain continues to fall
even as the sun slowly breaks through
The ghosts of remembrance
do not fade with the bugler's call

Still, we must remember

Canada's Weapon of War From Remembrance Day Onwards – Corinne Sawchuk

Canada had cruel weapons of war in World War I
With which to kill the conquering enemy,
Both sides to suffer casualties and deaths
For the sake of seeking victory in tanks
On foot, in trenches, or on warhorses with sabers.
They had land mines and mine detectors while wearing helmets.
They carried rifles with bayonets, fighting knives, swords,
Pistols sniper rifles, shotguns, and machine guns
with high explosive shells or star shells at nighttime.
They used delay-fuse, hand grenades,
Flame throwers, mortar bombs and poison gasses.
Overhead were huge Zeppelins and fighter planes.
On the sea were aircraft carriers and battleships,
With torpedoes and naval mines. Canada won that war!

Canada had crueler weapons of war in World War II
And used old and new ones to the maximum.
The tanks were bigger, 2 ½ ton truck could cross water
On its bottom while soldiers become tube breathers.
They wore lighter helmets and protective body armor.
They had recoilless rifles, submachine guns spraying bullets
Faster than from a pistol, self-loading and automatic guns,
Sniper scopes to see in the dark without being seen,
Rocket propelled grenades hand-held recoilless rocket launchers,
Being the Bazookas, tall ballistic weapons
The atomic bombs and depth charges. Canada won that war!

Canada had more cruel weapons of war in the Korean War.
The new ones were likely helicopters and destroyers –

Those small fast warships used to protect other ships
And destroy torpedo boats. Canada won that war!

Canada had more cruel weapons of war in two Gulf Wars.
Lazar-guided bombs followed by a dumb bomb
With a global positioning satellite (GPS),
Strategic bombers to do carpet-bombing,
Destroying everything within a mile long
And half a mile wide. Canada won that war!

Canada has more cruel weapons of war in Afghanistan
When Canada went there for peacekeeping purposes
Only to sometimes be faced with roadside bombs,
Booby traps, herbicides, blimps and drones.
They will leave weapons of mass destruction for there are
no winners.
As long as there are weapons of mass destruction,
There may not be any peace or winners in war.

Soldiers of War – Gary Redmond

Soldiers of War
Reminded with poppies
Why so many brave soldiers died
We stand silent each year
Our hearts open
Our eyes filled with tears

Planes fly by in unison
Our proud Canadians
Soldiers of war
Standing rank and file
They raise their rifles
Fire out loud
We salute you

Why for war?
For our country
For our family
For our home
All and more
Rest in peace
Brave soldiers of war

Your legacy
Lay in the soil
Of fields where poppies grow
Under a white cross
In rows upon rows
Lay to rest
But never alone

Lay so silent
But never forgotten
Without hate nor fear
Nor did they fight for glory
They fought for us
For peace not war

The Veteran's Call – John Athey
(Age 92)
One warm Canadian summer day,
Province of Ontario - 1938
My older brother read the paper,
and said-

"Seems they need help,
to keep the Empire free,
from Germany!"

"Maybe we should go and see,
what we might do
for our country."

He applied to the RCAF.
They return the request,

"From Germany, we are far away,
we may be interested
on a later day."

Brother Arther wrote the RAF
Canada still under the Royal Crown
 From the Brits, came a short communication
"Show up here in London,
And you can join the British Nation".

2 years older than me, age 19,
My brother working as apprentice,
at a flour and grain mill
away not far.

He saved his pennies
and brought himself a car.

Now he sold, the apple of his eyes,

And to his 29 Plymouth
He had to say goodbye.

With this pocket full of money,
we could try to make the trip
and turned to me, quite flip`

"I can pay your way, with what I saved,
quit school, and pay me back.
When you are in the RAF
and old enough to shave!"

So we hitched the 300 miles
to Montreal to learn
we could board a ship
$90.00 each, No Return!

Of course we were mere digits
in the volunteer vets of WW2
But We luckily survived the 7 years we gave,
to help save beautiful Canada
For me and you.

Whonnock Elementary School Poetry

My Dad – Silver Kuris
(1st place Elementary Category)

My daddy went to war today
Will anything ever be okay?
He hugged me close and blew a kiss
I treasure it so, because I know I will miss.

Everyday I pray to God,
To take care of my daddy so far abroad
That he will come home safe to me,
Can you hear my desperate plea?

I know my daddy is fighting for what's right
But I wish someone else would fight the fight
I just want him home safe with me
Do you think that could ever be?

Hope – Abby Puhl

Boom bang I look around me and what do I see
My teammates fighting to be free

Boom bank there goes a gun
I start to run

Over 6,000 passed away
I still believe that some did stay

Even though war still tries
I still believe that hope will rise.

War is the Worst – Teegan Fowle
(2nd place Elementary Category)

War is the worst,
Bombs will burst.

Soldiers will die
Families will cry.

Men steady their aim
Hoping they win but not for fame.

They hide behind the fences
And dig deep trenches.

Its muddy, rainy, dark. I hope this all ends soon
Almost every one I know has met their doom.

I look forward to the end of this
Because I don't want to be missed.

One Minute of Silence – Vanessa Schwarz

My country won
The war is done
A poppy I wear
Makes war seem so unfair

I can't imagine to lose your family
When you are supposed to live happily
They come home with bruises
While the other side loses

He keeps on running, he doesn't look back
The general will make a plan of attack
Those who lived packed their bags
And will raise their flags.

War is No Fun – Caleb Oneux

Man I see we war
I don't want to do this anymore

When I put on my boots
I hear a loud shoot

In World War One
It was no fun.

In war you fight
For your rights

In World War Two
There may be no more you.

War is no fun
Will it ever be done?

Peace – Brieanna Gough

Boom bang there goes a gun
The bombs weigh a ton

I see the sun
But its not fun

As my family runs
I'm left the only one.

The war has begun
Now I have to run.

World War I – Reece Selvey

War is scary you can die
There is a battle right before your eyes

Men shout battle cries
When bombs fly

The families part on bye
Soldiers go to war and the loved ones cry

Soldiers spy on the soldiers that lie
We are thankful for the ones that had to die.

I Shall Soon Join My Brothers – Antonio Tumaneng

Goodbye to my brothers
But I will see you again
The joys of heaven we will share
With the bless of our God there.

Families and friends wipe away the tears
All the killing and shooting, those were my fears
There should be no death nor pain
Most during the war go insane.

Goodbyes are not forever
Its only for a while
And when we get together
We'll share one big smile

I have some fond memories of the war
And I try hard not to grieve
I am tired and I want to die
I am ready to say my last goodbye.

I lifted my eyes to behold God
On that stormy night when none could see
But God overpowered all the darkness
His peace and love came over me.

Exchanging His love for my fears
He cured my heart, He set me free
I thought God didn't want me
Finally I'm with you ….. my brothers!

Dark and Dusty – Almea McLeod-Genest

Dark and dusty
Dusk to dawn
Waiting and wondering for no more gore to go on
The tanks have been released, the gun has been shot.
Now I regret to come and be the one.

Friends and family,
Duty to be done,
Muddy and dusty,
And the gore goes on.

Boom bank there goes a gun
I'm not the only one who thinks war is no fun,
Help me mom! Help me dad!
The war has just begun!

Life as a Soldier – Ethan Paulson

I lie in the trenches at risk of my life
How I have missed my children and wife
Boom! A bomb blows up in a field nearby
I shudder when I hear the cries of people nearby
I fight for Canada for freedom and right
The people struggle in the fight
Soldiers hide behind a tree
Soldiers are always ready for the enemy
A missile blows up a wall
This will be the last fall
There goes the last blast
The war has finally ended at last.

Made in the USA
Charleston, SC
16 November 2013